Baby Animals
of the North

Written and Illustrated
by Katy Main

ALASKA
NORTHWEST
BOOKS®

Blueberries are a favorite snack for this grizzly bear family. In the late summer, mother bear will show her cubs how to fish for salmon with their paws.

Sea otters like to eat clams, snails, worms, octopus, and starfish. Mother otter shows her baby how to break open a clam by banging the clam against a rock on her tummy.

To help them grow strong, mother wolf plays roughly with her five wolf pups.

Caribou calves will travel far and wide with
their mother and the rest of the herd to find
enough grass to eat.

Shy like their mother, these lynx kittens play near their den by day and prowl at night.

Even though this baby mountain goat is only a few hours old, it can already walk along a steep, rocky cliff.

Brown or gray in the summer, and white or blue in the winter, the beautiful fur of the mother arctic fox and her pups changes color through the seasons.

While her fawn nestles in a soft bed of leaves, mother Sitka deer checks to see that she is safe from danger.

After teaching her cubs
to climb trees to safety,
mother black bear rests
on a tree limb.

The long, shaggy hair of the musk oxen keeps them warm during winter's cold.

Up high, rocky mountains,
the Dall sheep climb to
find grasses they like to eat.
The lambs jump and frolic
on the rocks.

When coyote pups are first born, they stay in the den with their mother, while father coyote brings them food.

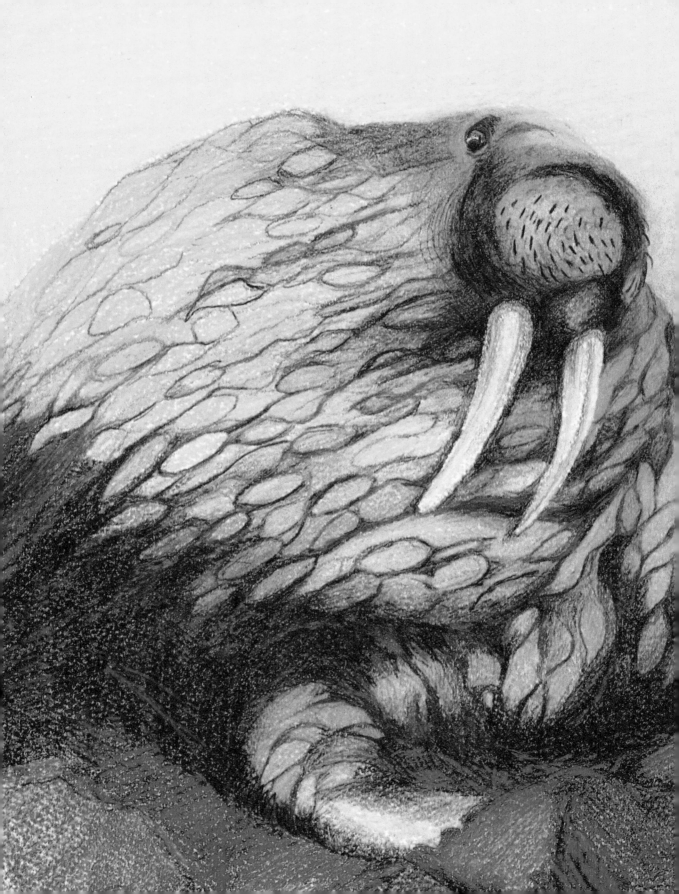

As walrus calves get older, their skin becomes wrinkled and tough, and they grow two white ivory tusks. They will use their tusks to pull themselves out of the water and onto the ice or the land.

For mother moose and her calves, long legs make it easy to wade into water in search of plants to eat.

When they aren't sleeping by their mother in the den, polar bear cubs sometimes swim with her in the water below the ice.

More about Baby Animals

Grizzly bears are born in late January or early February. Newborn cubs stay in the den with their mothers until April. Mother grizzlies nurse their cubs for one or two summers before sending them out on their own. Although grizzlies have no need to fear other animals, mother grizzlies must protect their young from adult male bears who, given the opportunity, will kill young cubs.

Sea otters spend much of their time cleaning and grooming their fur in order to keep warm and to prevent water from touching their skin. Sea otter pups are born year-round. Unable to dive for food, a newborn pup will spend its first three months on his mother's chest, nursing frequently.

Wolves commonly live, travel, and hunt in groups called packs. A pack generally has six to eight members, and usually consists of a group of animals that are related to each other by blood. Wolf pups are born in May in litters of two to thirteen pups. Helpless at birth, pups remain in the den with their mothers for their first month of life. When they leave the den, the other members of the pack share the job of protecting, feeding, and teaching the pups to hunt.

Caribou are often called the "nomads of the north" because they are constantly on the move in search of food. Male and female caribou have antlers, though the antlers of a bull are larger and more massive than those of a cow. Caribou calves are born in late May or early June. Within minutes of birth, calves can stand and walk, but are easy prey for wolves and bears.

Lynx are shy animals that generally hunt and travel at night. Lynx kittens are born in a den, which may be a hollow log or pile of brush, and remain with their mother well into their first winter. The snowshoe hare provides the main source of food for lynx.

Mountain goats inhabit the windswept ridges and alpine meadows of the mountains in south and southeastern Alaska. Cushioned skid-proof pads on their hooves provide traction and grip for climbing steep and rocky surfaces. Born in May or June, mountain goat kids and their nannies (or mothers) group together to form nursery flocks.

Arctic foxes are small, weighing only about twelve pounds when fully grown. Found mostly along the Arctic coast, these animals are valued by humans for their fur. Fox pups are born in a den during May or June and remain in the den until fall, when they strike out on their own.

Sitka deer are born during the month of May or June. Fawns are reddish-brown in color, with random spots of white on their sides. The spots begin to disappear by September. In winter, their reddish-brown coat changes to dark gray.

Black bears aren't necessarily black. They can be brown, or cinnamon-colored, or even blue-gray. Black bear cubs are born in dens in January or February and remain there until April or May. Mothers nurse their young for about eight months and teach their cubs how to hunt, where to den, and what to eat. The family hibernates together for the cubs' first winter. The following spring the cubs leave their mother and go out on their own.

Iñupiaq Eskimos call **musk oxen** *oomingmak* or "bearded one." During the spring and summer, these shaggy, hump-shouldered animals shed their long winter undercoat. The fur is gathered to make yarn for sweaters, scarves, and hats. Early whalers and traders hunted musk oxen for food and for their fur. In Alaska, the last surviving musk oxen were killed in 1865. Musk oxen from Greenland were successfully reintroduced to Alaska in the 1930s.

Dall sheep are known for their striking white coat and distinctive curled horns. Dall sheep lambs are born in May or June and can walk quite well within a few hours of birth. By the time they are a week old, they walk sure-footedly behind their mother on steep, rocky cliffs.

Coyotes are members of the dog family. Pups are born in a den during the spring, usually in litters of five to seven pups. Both father and mother coyotes bring the pups food and teach them how to stalk and hunt for food. In the fall, the pups are ready to go out on their own.

Walrus calves are dependent on their mother for their first eighteen months. Weighing from 85 to 140 pounds at birth, walruses can grow to be eight to ten feet long and weigh one to two tons as adults. The long ivory tusks of the walrus are used to maneuver their massive bodies out of the water. Eskimos traditionally hunted the walrus, using the meat for food, the skins for making boats, and the ivory for making tools and decorative objects.

Moose are the largest members of the deer family and are distinguished by their size (up to 1,600 pounds for bulls), long neck, and drooping nose. Moose calves are born in late May or early June, often in swampy muskegs, and remain with their mothers through their first winter. Mother cows fiercely defend their young. Only bull moose grow antlers, which grow up to six feet from tip to tip and which they shed every year.

Polar bears live on the ice cap of the Far North. The largest of all bears, polar bears can reach eight to ten feet in length and weigh up to 1,200 pounds. At birth, cubs weigh only about a pound. Cubs are born in December in dens, where they live with their mother until the spring.

**To my mother, Irene,
who made children's books
come alive for me.**

Text and illustrations © 1992 by Katy Main

Library of Congress Catalog Card Number: 91-78180

ISBN: 978-1-941821-51-0 (softbound)
ISBN: 978-1-943328-11-6 (hardbound)

Published by Alaska Northwest Books®
An imprint of

GRAPHIC ARTS
BOOKS®

P.O. Box 56118
Portland, Oregon 97238-6118
503-254-5591
www.graphicartsbooks.com

CPSIA information can be obtained
at www.ICGtesting.com
Printed in the USA
LVOW05s2302080516

487277LV00007B/12/P

9 781941 821510